LIFE IS CRYING

Greeting Maryann,

Much joy and happiness wishes for you.

you are appreciated

Benjana Brown

LIFE IS CRYING

BENZENA BROWN

NIESHA BATTLE • SADEJA GRIFFIN

Palmetto Publishing Group
Charleston, SC

Life Is Crying
Copyright © 2020 by Benzena Brown, Niesha Battle,
and Sadeja Griffin

First Edition

Printed in the United States

ISBN-13: 978-1-64111-984-9
ISBN-10: 1-64111-984-5

I am consumed with grieving sorrow

Risk of overdose
Habit forming
Supplier of multiple health issues
Travels world wide
Life's pleasure imposter

WANTED

Sharp piercing blade that stabs the mind/brain
Considered a serial killer
Interrupts life survival
and
Destroys a healthy lifestyle

Warning

Dangerous and fierce: Will hook and possess victims' lives
Armed with destructive, sensational, and delightful pleasures that really
get a hold on you
Ruthless Giant that will invade and alter the mind/behavior

Destroyer

Brutal to life survival
Hijacker and manipulator of the brain
If used, be prepared to suffer turmoil, agony, and tragedy

**For information and assistance, call the National Drug Line:
844-433-8400**

ACKNOWLEDGEMENTS

Barbara Ellis, who encouraged me to write

Eldridge Cleaver, author of *Soul on Ice*,
who encouraged me to write

My mother, Clementine Brown

My father, Benjamin Brown

My aunts, Mary Slaughter and Shirley Langford

My fifth-grade teacher, Mrs. Stevenson,
sister of Count Basis

Duane Miller, teacher and mentor

Colorado Barrett

Dedicated to My Beloved Grandson-
who brought me joy

And my siblings who always offer me support

CONTENTS

AUTHOR'S NOTE

In loving memory of my only brother, a prominent businessman, who had a chemical dependency addiction. My brother was sober for approximately twenty-five years and succumbed to drug addiction after a prolonged absence from drugs. Chilling and disturbing alert which trust was undoubtedly a mistake. During his period of addiction, he intentionally burned his nephew with an iron leaving a lifetime scar. He also forced him to eat his morning cereal with kool-aid.

My influence for writing this book is love, exposure, challenge, pain, suffering, and experiences from close family members and acquaintances addicted to drugs. The battlefield for survival and sobriety is challenging, is heartbreaking, and is flooded with tears and pain; however, it can be conquered with recovery support, a strong and determined desire, and the will to make it happen by believing you can. Drugs are weapons when abused, with results leading to chemical dependency, which robs and destroys the foundation and structure of life and survival. Drugs do not discriminate; however, the medical attention and justice system give disparate treatment to individuals of color who are addicted to drugs.

> *I can do all things through Christ who*
> *strengthens me.*
> —Philippians 4:13 (KJV)

Chemical dependency is personal to me, and accordingly, I will try to inform others and especially youth on dangers and warn potential and new users of side effects. Please beware; your life is at stake.

This book is written and designed to provide information about chemical dependency and drugs, and the drug gives its message to you! The book is written to persuade, influence, surrender, and conquer challenges associated with chemical dependency.

To all who have survived the parasite and allergy of addiction and recovered to a normal, productive life with their families, congratulations!

To all who are struggling and fighting the battle of addiction, support is available.

To all who are challenged with addiction and do not understand how to get help and what to do, help is available.

To all who are family or friends seeking or offer loving support and becoming frustrated add loving support– and feeling helpless, help is available.

Remembering those who were stuck in the wilderness and lost their lives to overdoses—we forgive and remember with love.

To all who have learned to take one day at a time to enjoy a fulfilling life, recovery is continuous action. Congratulations!

Love and respect to all, filled with prayers, help, healing, and high hopes.

PREFACE

Universal Outcry: Help, Hope, and Healing Blasting the Grip of Destruction!

Chemical dependency is crippling, deadly, and harmful, and statistics of victims are rapidly increasing. Some of victims develop a chemical dependency beginning in youth. The results are an interrupted and uncomfortable life for the victim, family, friends, work, social interaction, employment, life skills, and communication. Life is crying for sobriety. On observation of number of medical hospitals, leading are chemical dependency recovery centers and clinics in the number of facilities offering service. What an outcry—because many suffering from chemical dependency are without treatment.

Chemical dependency is defined as a drug addiction that is chronic and a mental illness. Drug addiction cause compulsive, repetitive craving, drug seeking and use, despite harmful consequences to the addict Chemical dependency addiction is also considered a complex brain disorder, a mental illness, and a relapsing brain disease. The results are a habit of intensive craving and use of the drug.

Addiction is also associated and linked with the term "allergy." An allergy is an allergic reaction that causes the body's response to become negative or unmanageable. For instance, if an individual has a negative response to strawberries each time they are consumed, the allergy will surface. Normally, an individual will stop eating strawberries to avoid negative consequences. This negative reaction exists even when they are not eating strawberries. An allergy is automatically activated by the consumption of strawberries. Body will always react negatively with consequences each time strawberries are consumed. Addiction and substance abuse follow the principle of an allergy and react negatively with consequences when a drug is consumed. A chemical dependency allergy is similar to being on a leash. On a leash you are choked, pulled, and direct by the controller of the leash. A chemical dependency allergy will control you like being on a leash.

A chemical dependency causes life's foundation to become uncontrollable, and the ability to manage foundation of life skills becomes impaired and needs help. The pleasure of addiction screams in agony flooded with tears and helplessness, while choking sobs flow for the escape of the drug. The pleasure of a chemical dependency addiction dominates the cry of helplessness. The emotion of survival is a continuous streak of destructive behavior, all for the pleasure of the drug. Trying to escape the craving and allergic reactions of addiction is a barrier that does not seem to let go of the victim unless it is treated and the victim becomes rehabilitated.

Rehabilitation may be inpatient or outpatient in a professional treatment faculty whose goal is prevention oriented, referring to drug addiction. Rehabilitation is defined as restoring an individual to health or a normal life through training with a counselor, group therapy, individual therapy, and/or a physician. The goal is to assist the individual to understand and apply productive and healthy life skills after imprisonment, addiction, or an illness. Education is a source for answers in understanding addiction and its consequences. Recovery or rehabilitation is like a lit candle; blow out the fire/flame, and you lose the burning mode.

> *Broken crayons still color.*
> —Dr. Dale Bonner

This means that restoration is possible and a productive life can be restored with support. Drug addiction may require that an individual be detoxed. Detoxing is process that removes or rids the body of toxic or unhealthy substances. Sobriety is about getting and keeping toxic crap out; it stinks! The content of an abused substance dwells like an infectious wound filled with bacteria; it's a destruction to the body and mind. Chemical dependency is as dreadful as a lion, eager to tear and rip his prey. Sobriety is the state of being sober, alert, focused, and drug-free.

The outcry is real and devastating, do not discriminate, and the outcry is universal. Chemical dependency's universal groan and sigh is "Please release me." Chemical dependency is a sticking hold and a gripping destabilizing fuel. Chemical dependency is also labeled as a mental disorder, and according to the National Alliance on Mental Illness (NAMI), mental illness is the third most common cause of hospitalization in the United States.

Thought for consideration: The most valuable asset you carry everywhere you are is your life. Do not wreck life with harmful drugs. Take the elevator up a level at a time, and set goals.

DEDICATION TO MY GRANDSON

Loving You Thru Fond Memories and
A Spiritual Bond and Connection

Tragic interruptions are the hardest and most painful. Yes, I am experiencing a choking and a stomach boiling sensation because you are gone. Tears will not bring you back or give me comfort. I love you!

Living on forbidden ground is what seem to bring you comfort and pleasure. Forbidden ground brought me sorrow. My life will change. I am now experiencing anguish of being in a maze. Drugs took you away and my heart cannot escape the pain. Forbidden ground is chemical dependency and the power of pleasure its' has on life.

You tried to escape alone. Drugs became your battle field and my devastating acceptance. Trying to help you without returns, strike me with depression and sleepless days and nights.

I believe in God and pray that we will hug each other tight when I join you. I love you and that love for you is endless. Be grateful and thankful, I am grateful and thankful for your life spent with me. I will keep fond memories of you!

You will never depart from me because of the love; I share for you within my heart.

DEDICATION LETTER OF LOVE AND SORROW

To: My Favorite Beloved Cousin

I am a custom to writing to you with the expectation of receiving a letter back. Today, I am writing my last letter to you. I am heartbroken going through memories. Did you know we have so many positive memories? Its' been two days and I have not had the same memory twice.

I knew you were dealing with something that was bigger than we could ever try to fix. We complimented each other so well because we both struggled with mental health. We tried self- medicating while trying to care for each other with the intention of not making each other feel worst. I love you for caring about me; when I tried to commit suicide.

No one knew how sensitive you were. You had hope in hopeless situations. I wish you had continued to stay with us and never moved to your mom's house. Somewhere down the road between losing your friend and moving to your Mothers' I felt your soul leaving. I cried. I wish we could have helped each other be healthy and productive.

The hole you dug eventually consumed you and I struggled. I know if we were on the phone right now, I will tell you how my life is going and the changes I made to improve my life. You loved hearing about sobriety. I haven't done meth in months and I haven't tried killing myself in a long time. I am going back to college. Taking care of my mental illness until the day I die.

You did not deserve to die in an alley alone missing. I am paralyzed in my thoughts and emotions. Missing you is an understatement. I haven't eaten or slept well in days. You occupy my mind, heart and soul. You will live eternally through me. I will never forget you and the role you played in my life.

P.S. I love you my favorite cousin!

PART ONE:

Chemical Dependency/Substance Abuse

INTRODUCTION

Defeat Me if You Can! Drug Addiction- Crippling, Clinging and Gripping Motto:

I will hook you until you can let me go. I will make your life like a tug-of-war that ripples and is tormented with bruises and crises. These are my confessions and testimonies to you! Just like the sky, people, illness, life, death, money, day, and night, I am wide spread all over the world! I am your pleasure pimp! I am chemical dependency a ruthless giant!

Chemical dependency, I am your master and expert of drug addiction. Listen to me. This is my message; I speak to you! I will hook you until you can let me go! Listen to me; I am speaking truth to you. I am exposing my life's aim and actions to you. I will live within your mind and body as a parasite with an allergic reaction. I come in many forms. I am a drug designed to addict you. I can be sniffed, you can drink me, you may take me intravenously or even smoke me if you choose—the choice is yours. I will lift you up, and you will consider it fun; however, there is a fall of pain like falling naked into a train filled with a ton of bricks falling and striking you at a high speed. I am alcohol, methamphetamine, cocaine, heroin, opioids, and drugs that create unmanageable, uncontrollable, harmful side effects.

The pleasure of addiction shines like rays of bright sunshine, while the battle of addiction sparks and sparkles with delays like shooting beams of flashing lights switching off and on, and focus becomes like falling stars. Thorns of addiction scream and shout, "I will pinch you. I will stick you, and I can make you bleed and give you pain!" I am capable of killing you while making you smile and laugh. You will seek and crave me. I will make you scream, cry, steal, and destroy your family and home. You will become homeless and have the possibility of jail or prison, and you still will not let me go. You and your family will experience pain and helplessness as I possess your life. I will ruin your family values, influence lies, and make lies your paradise until you let me go and defeat me.

Loyalty, what is it? I am your number-one love, and you have been robbed of loyalty, and still you seek me and keep coming back. I am powerful. I am an addiction, and I can make you come running back to me when you try to defeat me. I am like a poisonous snake. I will make you fall when I strike, and there is a definite need for treatment, just like venom from a snakebite to survive and defeat me.

When becoming homeless, my victims in freezing-cold weather have climbed to rooftops seeking and hoping to get warmth from the heat rising within a residence or facility but still cling to me and crave me and will not let me go. I am a master drug of chemical dependency addiction and can control you. I will make you chase me like a team of wild horses, galloping and lost in the wilderness, and still you cling to me and will not let me go.

You can deny me if you choose. I will put you on your knees, crying, screaming, and asking for help despite your denial until you let me go and defeat me.

You are my eggshell. I will make you fragile, and you will crack. The *D* in chemical dependency drugs symbolizes danger, damage, and destruction. I have no physical or mental limitation on my aim to conquer you. Victory is my aim to conquer you, and you will become my prisoner.

I will hook you until you can defeat me and let me go.

I am in control of your goals, your life, and your behavior, and I have your mind in a state of confusion. I can terminate your business and destroy employment, making you jobless, and still you cannot let me go.

My side effects for your life are low esteem, mental and physical dysfunction, terminal illness, and even death, and you keep coming back, seeking me. I love to freak you out with illusions and make you feel breathless until I can take your breath away. Tackle me and I will strike back; you are in my custody. I am your prison; I will not break the chain. Your freedom is mine, and still you keep craving and seeking me.

I will strangle you in detox without hands or substance. You will suffer pain, shivering, trembling, nausea, fatigue, weakness, and still you will not let me go.

I will make you sink like quicksand, pulling you down with great force as you scream with your hands up to avoid the sink—"Help, help, help!"—while trying to get free, unless you defeat me and let me go.

Some take advantage of my services, knowing you are becoming a priority emergency candidate of death row. I am sold for profit and wealth; however, my profit makers are not drug users. Money is their aim.

I can become very expensive and rob you of all assets, regardless of your wealth, resources, or assets. I will make your life crumble like toasted bread crumbs and cookie crumbs as it falls apart and shrinks to disaster. The life and craving of chemical dependency addiction may be encountered as scolding hot water eating your flesh away. You will experience your body feeling like nails being hammered in your body, preparing you for burial.

I can become your companion like the blood flowing through your veins and heart and the air you breathe; however, my mission is not lifesaving but life destruction.

All of you with minor children, beware: child protective services will be doing their job.

How do you break my chain? Acknowledge the need for help and support with determination, choices, and will, believing you can conquer with victory. Get help and support!

> *And the prayer of faith will save the sick, and the Lord will raise him up. And if he has committed sins, he will be forgiven.*
> —James 5:15 (KJV)

This is my true story. I am a drug addiction, and I will possess your life and fill it with agony, sorrow, grief, and even possibly death. The fact is, it doesn't matter where you come from; what matters is what you do and what vision you have. What you do is determined by your thoughts and actions. I am your demon and will fill your life with chaos. My life fact is being a simulant drug. I mess with your brain receptor and signals. For instance, I transmit messages similar to the transmission of text messages on your cell phone to reach your recipient; my drug transmissions reach your brain.

Believe my messages to you. My side effects are sensationally pleasure based, leading to disastrous, devastating pain, and I can lead to overdose and even death. Defeat me if you will!

We are celebrities because we are famous, entertained, and known all over the world for our pleasure, our fallen ones, our families, and our addicted. In every scene of your life, you have a choice. Make a good one!

Life Is Crying

The Dilemma of Chemical Dependency Sabotage

The blade that stabs the mind/brain

Help
Screaming-Choking

Help   *Help*
Painful Sobs *Panic*

Help   *Help*
Health Issues   *Disparate Treatment*

Help   **Universal**   *Help*
Imprisoned   **Outcry**   *Family Support*

Help   *Help*
Financial Burden   *Family Division*

Help   *Help*   *Help*   *Help*
Overdose   *Relapse*   *Offers Outreach*   *Behavior Crisis*

CLIMBING OUT OF A PIT LESS FALL

Scared, trapped—a wrecking rerun chain of torment events. Drugs and guns are destructive to survival; and are at risk of the paralyzing phenomenon of hostages' terror.

Alert! Life is crying gigantic sobs of despair and grief. Drugs are everywhere. My head is shaking no in disgust while my heart is pounding with sorrow. This universal phenomenon of drugs and addiction is striking my loved one. Shaking my head no is in recognition of this believable reality that was unbelievable to me and a decay to life.

I am a mother and grandmother, and out of helplessness due to rules, I watched my loved one struggle with addiction. Is this a result of a lost connection of guidance or influence by other factors unknown to me? I suffered, trying to understand this phenomenal pit that controls one's life and conquers one's mindset.

When and how did this happen? Many dreadful series of events, throbbing chokes of sorrow, become like a flood from a hurricane consisting of a flashing, cracking, stretching reach of lightning and booming, cracking sound of thunder.

He was a child and was introduced to drugs. A child whose decision-making was developing, not matured enough to understand the effects of drugs. My thoughts were that he was a middle-school youth who was in school, learning and excited about recreation, video games, sports, and cartoons. Yes, choices are a decision; however, life skills for decision-making are a learned process of development.

My sibling as a youth was at risk, and I did not realize it. He lived a double life between his parents. The parents were young, and parental skills were undeveloped. In fact, the mother resented the father and made it public information.

Money begin going missing from my purse. Believing that no one in the household would take my money, I blamed myself for misplacing the money. Stealing did not stop with money being missing; other items of value began going missing. Ignoring and justifying a valid action of discovery is an error of consequence with negative side effects. Wrongdoing is not corrected by ignoring an action with an invalid excuse of self-blame. My actions were symbolic of trust, which is needed; however, when a problem arises, consequences surface, and trust is limited or violated.

A lack of interest in school and disrespect of family began to surface. A lack of performing tasks, sleeping for extended periods, telling lies, having illusions, hiding in dark closets, being untidy, and having confrontations were frequent behavior traits. His education suffered with being absent from school for prolonged periods. As he grew into a young man, his drug habit grew with him. His appearance became frightening. Time was served in prison for stealing. When he was released from prison, I was thrilled and believed he had learned his lesson. Many broken promises were made while he was in prison. Entering society and being rejected for employment and other interests led to depression and drugs again. Yes, he searched for employment, and parole officers seem to hammer his esteem.

Soon he was using drugs again like drinking water. Addicts were sneaking into my house though the bedroom window, and I was terrified. I did not want to send my loved one back to prison. I went to casinos to escape the turmoil and even sat at a bus stop all night one night. I felt I was in the middle, trying to provide what I thought my loved one was missing. I was accused of not doing enough; however, I was doing all I knew how to do.

My loved one became an embarrassment to many family members, and contact with him was avoided. It was as though he had become a human beast with a contagious disease. "Kick him out of our lives" seemed to be the family attitude. His behavior was too much for us to bear. I wanted to save my loved one; his addiction was greater and more powerful than me or my knowledge. My life was hell as things worsened. I listen to recovering addicts express actions and say that hitting rock bottom is necessary for the addict to change. Well, I do not have a chemical dependency; however, I was hitting rock bottom. Hitting rock bottom for me felt like shoveling melting snow and expecting to create a snowman. We both were living in bondage. My emotional bondage was like a sharpened ax hitting a tree stump, blocking the road, comparable to blocking a desire for recovery.

Holiday time and family gatherings came. My family prepared a Thanksgiving feast, and we went, expecting family fun. Greeted with smiles, I was ready for good food and family stories. My loved one walked in last. He was not high; however, the tension in the room was thicker than blinding fog. Family departed the room and did not return. We waited for approximately an hour.

The food was on the table, so we ate and left without the remaining family joining us for the feast.

Arriving home, my sibling approached his father, asking to live with him. My sibling's father agreed, and they left on Thanksgiving Night. I felt relief. The rule of my house is that when you are high, you do not come here. When he was high and it was cold outside, he claims he slept on rooftops for warmth. Things did not change in my sibling's father's residence. In fact, my sibling had to move because of his son's behavior.

His mother blamed us until she experienced the same outcome. Leaving his mother's home, he was found naked, slapped with bruises, and scarred with challenges of becoming homeless. I was called and asked the person who found him to take him to the hospital. The hospital transferred him to a mental health facility. I was relieved he was now in a mental health facility, and treatment begin; he was unhappy. I prayed, I prayed, and I prayed. Each traumatizing challenge elevated daily.

> *Now faith is the substance of things hoped for,*
> *the evidence of things unseen.*
> —Hebrews 11:1(KJV)

I continued to pray, despite the journey filled with toxic behavior and heartbreaking trauma.

Pray without ceasing.
—1 Thessalonians 5:17(KJV)

Currently, we are still fighting the battle.

CHEMICAL DEPENDENCY ADDICTION

It is a significant or compulsive craving contributing to the habit of dependency despite harmful consequences. It's a claw effect! I am your hatchet! I am your brain tweeter. I can and will hold you hostage! Defeat me if you can!

Chemical dependency is continuous use of a substance and the inability to stop using the drug or control the use of the drug. Chemical dependency is referred to as an addiction. The body develops a hunger known as a craving for the substance. Without the substance, the body feels starved and hungers for or craves the drug. The drug grabs with stings and claws, leading to dependency on the drug like a net full of crab claws wrapped in a net with you. You are tumbling and fighting to get out, and the crab claws in the net will not let go.

The mental health district becomes your residence if you are lucky. It's a shivering effect. You have lost control and cannot manage without the drug. Jail, prison, and homelessness become shelters. Even begging sometimes plays its role in addiction's life. Life is crying on your behalf; however, you are too consumed with the drug to notice. Chemical dependency will take you to the dreadful corner of being broke—broke without money, broke without self-love and family, broke without being alert, broke without a residence, broke without joy in life, broke without resources. Your state is limited to drug-survival life. Drug-survival life will introduce you to depression, anxiety, anger, domestic violence, loneliness, tooth decay, and even death. Your consciousness has faded to illusions and blackouts, and you become doomed. The body is suffering from self-inflicted brutality.

The love for self and family has now become like junk and has been trashed. Addiction is one of the hardest roads to travel. The road is filled with the pleasure of the drug first; then it advances to torment and is a highway to hell.

Help is available, and getting help does not always come easily. There is an issue with relapse and availability. The strain to be sober again requires work, and it may seem out of reach. The most reliable method is to take heed and stay away from harmful drugs.

If you are trapped in a claw's net, the net has holes; free yourself. Begin a program such as outpatient care. Have a healthy life again. Life skills training is available. Remove life trauma on chemical dependency, or go to inpatient care, depending on your assets. Also, free help is available. You can survive chemical dependency; sobriety's side effect is a healthy life. Dwell with help, hope, and healing.

Chemical dependency will take you to a road of being desperate and will financially ruin you. It will rob you of life; it consumes you and can lead to destruction with consequences and no positive productive actions! Chemical dependency is a slain destroyer of life.

Addiction is a tug-of-war. Experiencing a tug-of-war chemical dependency will keep you falling down. The well-being of your health will begin to deteriorate, and your physical and mental states become disabled. Infectious wounds are bacteria filled and are painful and require medical care; it is likewise for a body being tormented with substance abuse. Additionally, the brain is impacted from substance abuse, and a highly pleasurable sensation is experienced. This experience medically is known as a euphoric feeling. A euphoric feeling simply is a powerful and intense sensational feeling of excitement and happiness. A powerful grip and intense urgency is triggered for the sensation of excitement and happiness experienced, which is referred to as "chasing the dragon." The hook of chasing the dragon is related to the neurotransmitter dopamine. Dopamine is responsible for transmitting signals between the nerve cells and brain. A powerful grip keeps you coming back for the highly pleasurable sensation because the sensation time is short, but the urgency for the sensation can be lifelong and destructive. The time span of the pleasure and sensation of happiness normally does not exceed thirty minutes; torment is timeless. Money is one of the most used commodities all around the world, and chemical dependency is becoming number two. Digest this. You see, chemical dependency is widespread and popular just like money. I am your drug-addiction substance manipulator with a shotgun aimed at your life, and the trigger is being pulled. The bullets are set, and you lack a shield to protect you. Pain has no preference; pains afflicts everyone in some form eventually. Chemical dependency states, "Once we have developed an intimate relationship, you will discover I am not a pain reliever; I am a pain inflictor."

Defeat me if you will! I am your pleasure pimp and the blade that stabs the mind! It a mouse trap, and you can get free. Become an agent of hope. Be still; there is a light in the clouds.

Mouse Trap

Trapped, struggling for escape

CURIOSITY,
RING THE BELL

Drug addiction curiosity's confession:
Hear me, hear me, hear me! Seeking life
pleasure? Try out how sweet I am to please you.
My goal is to keep you coming back. I am legal
and can be harmful. I can give you disturbing
thoughts and behavior.. I can keep you coming
back. I can hook you with pleasure.
The outcome are severe consequences. It's your
future; dive in it with confidence. Knowledge,
growth, learning, and purpose are filled with
benefits and resources.

Hello, I am alcohol. Many love me, and I can become the number-one love of your life. Although, I am a legal drug, I am not harmless.

Ding-dong, ding-dong, ding-dong. I am giving you facts about myself, alcohol chemical dependency addiction. Curiosity is my meal and feast of attraction to get you hooked. Your peers love me, and you are convinced you should try me. Do not ignore me; you will acquire a craving for me, yearning and wondering about me. Thoughts will stick in your mind for me like superglue. I strangled you with my taste in the beginning, sometimes choking and coughing, a hint of what I am capable of doing to your life. I am alcohol. I am known and sought by every culture, male or female. Yes, I am famous, and many fall in love with me. My availability is from sunrise to sunset. I deserve a star for fame.

The drama of drowning in curiosity can be linked to peer pressure, stress, lack of knowledge, depression, acceptance, rejection, and lack of wisdom and understanding the link and connection to acquiring the hazardous risk of alcoholism.

> *Wisdom is the principle* thing; *Therefore, get wisdom. And in all your getting, get understanding.*
> —Proverbs 4:2 (KJV)

Behavior, character changes, and personality changes begin to surface. You and I have become like best friends or buddies; however, the missing factor is that a friend offers loving support. I offer my control of you with craving, urgency, and priority. Curiosity now has you caught up in a love triangle. It's me that you seek; love for me, alcohol, has its ties and loose ends wrapped in knots. I become your jewelry box, and you fill me with alcohol, your treasured desire.

Confession and justification of the relaxation game are no longer valid for consumption. You lack control of and cannot manage craving for me. You hide me and think family and friends are unaware that you have me hidden in a secret place.

Your shivers, shakes, eyes, voice, inability to walk and stand, blackouts, fatigue, and drowsiness are not easily hidden. The results are in, and I find you in my possession for consumption in life daily and frequently. The key factor for you and I, alcohol, is that we have started to share a secret life together as your thoughts cling to alcohol.

CAUGHT BY SURPRISE

Happy hour, the place for engagement of laughter. Fun and drinking are promotional acceptance.

The popularity of happy hour is as popular as payday. It seems everyone enjoys and desires happy hour like it is a payday.

Yes, yes, yes! You are of legal age to enjoy and join the fun. If you think coffee is the number-one drink, look at the shelves in grocery stores. Alcohol outnumber the coffee shelves' stock and other store beverages by giant spaces. Alcohol stock is almost everywhere: liquor stores, corner stores, markets, casinos, restaurants, bars, parties, concerts, pubs, and dinners. It may be labeled as a popular drink. Pay attention. Alcohol is promoted to get your attention with happy faces, smiles, appearances of fun times, party scenes, and social gathering. In the beginning, alcohol can be pleasurable, socially or casually;

however, if alcohol becomes your frequent and everyday companion and you depend on alcohol, consumption will become a problem and will develop issues in your life. You are now a part of a universal outcry, grabbing any opportunity to have your next drink, whether secretly or sociably. Intoxication from drinking consumption begins to strike life, and life functions negatively.

Side effects experienced include blackouts, memory loss, staggering and trying to walk straight (while you fall and pretend or think you are walking straight), slurred speech, headaches, pain, body aches, vomiting, tiredness or fatigue, and a body's reluctance to move. This is known as a hangover, which feels as though another drink is an answer. Even though you may vomit and feel you are damaging your intestines, you love me and find a way to have another drink, regardless of my harm to you and your body.

Many try to disguise issues with the consumption of alcohol, and alcohol becomes a part of a secret life. It is declared by an overwhelming number of alcohol consumers: "I can quit whenever I want." This neglects to confront a consumption problem that may exist. Alcohol can be thought of as a creepy crawler; the power in its grasp will hook you before you become aware of its potency.

Do not drive a car; you will risk an accident and possibly injure or kill others or even yourself. The legal consumption drinking level is less than .08 percent. Drinking and driving is a violation of law and may result in jail or even prison, emotional damage, physical and mental distress, and a possible lawsuit.

I am alcohol; your consumption is critical for controlling and managing me. I frequently celebrate the arrival of a new companion as I am consumed, and many start to drink in excess. Influences include but are not limited to:

- Peer pressure
- Social gatherings
- Parties
- Availability
- Exposure
- Curiosity
- Habits
- Focus

My rap song:

Set Me Free
Set me, set me, set me free
I say you really put a hold on me
Yes, you really put a hurt on me
Yeah, yeah, yeah
I don't like you being trapped by me, but you love me
you are always thinking of me
Yes, I treat you badly
you must defeat me and stop craving me
However, I still love you madly,
I don't want to lose you, because you need me
Don't want to blame you, but you needed me
Your love is strong now— I really put a hold on you
How can you release me, say goodbye, and let you me
go?
I want to leave you, don't want to stay here
Don't want to spend another day here
Wasting my time, destroying my mind
Shattering my life, limiting my skills
Bombarding my knowledge
Oh, oh, oh, yes, I want to split…
And set myself free
These chemical substances are killing me
Yes, you really put a hurt on me

However, you can break away
And flee
From the grip of chemical dependency
And be set free, no more having hurt put on you
No more trapping you!
You see the light shining through the clouds
You are set free

There is a rainbow in the storm

CELEBRATION TIME: I AM ALCOHOL

I am legal; my only restriction is your age. I can cause blackouts and memory loss with excessive and frequent consumption. Intoxication, do not fret. I can take you there. I am your roller coaster of thrills and tears!

Celebration time is for holidays, parties, sports games of favorite teams, gambling, special occasions, dates, picnics, birthdays, and just-because times. Celebrations are a part of every culture. It is normally viewed as a fun time. Many times, fun times are accompanied with alcohol. Alcohol and the sounds of music can make celebrations wild and extravagant events. Music and alcohol become like an electric switch; it can be turned on by me, alcohol. Singing, dancing, foot stomping, hand clapping, head nodding, shoulder bopping. Touch us, and ignite a special mood to enjoy an experience of music, food, and alcoholic pleasure. Enjoying social gatherings for many is just not enough. It seems that many times, I, alcohol am invited to the party. I guess you can say that I am the life of the party. Regardless, laughter and dancing and social interactions seem to liven up with my presence and consumption.

Social invitations solicit your presence with food, activities, music, and friends' outreach. Wow, did they forget to mention me? I am the special quest to liven the event. Most know me, alcohol, and expect to enjoy my presence. I am the booze sting of a celebration.

I am also a profit and investment resource. For instance, bars, many restaurants, casinos, markets, and liquor stores are very profitable when they sponsor me. Casinos offers gifts to reach customers weekly. The biggest of their offers is alcohol; they silently promote me. I am available twenty-four hours a day and seven days a week. Now, which promotion do you think is the most profitable? I know it! Me, alcohol! Profit and promotion are acquired not by the selling of alcohol but by the serving of alcohol twenty-fours a day, seven days a week. It's one of the casinos' business hacks.

Prevailing laws govern the intake of how much consumption of me, alcohol, is considered a risk to your life and others when driving. Some of these laws only the wealthy can survive. My recommendation is rule one: do not drink me, alcohol, and drive, which I do agree with. Rule two, do not drink me, alcohol, and fight; it is a risky lost, costly financial risk and is threatening to your well-being. Acquiring a criminal background is treated as a bashing stone, especially for minorities.

I, alcohol, cannot recall alcohol-based businesses going out of business. Normally, the supply of me is unlimited because the demand for supply of me is not limited. It's business, and it sells every day. People shop for me like buying groceries or dining at their favorite restaurant or fast-food dwelling.

HANGOVER ALCOHOL SYNDROME

Oh, what a crisis of pain it is! The side effects bear consequences of being sick and tired.

Ha, ha, ha. It's me, alcohol hangover syndrome. Oh no, it feels like I have a fire burning through my head that cannot be put out. What a pain, the hangover. I can't get up. My eyes are red and blurred. I feel sick, and my body is tired. My body aches like french fries sizzling in scolding hot oil. Ouch, what a pain it is. "Ouch" is not a strong enough expression. So I scream! Damn. Is the toenail fungus vomiting too? I am sick, screaming, "Oh no, my head cannot handle it! It's spinning and blazing like fire."

Well, you are feeling the side effects of drinking excessive amounts of alcohol, referred to as an intoxication hangover. Alcohol is labeled as the gateway to addiction and may lead to other drugs. *The Lancet* Medical Journal advises that alcohol increases the risk of hypertension, stroke, and heart attack.

> *It is good neither to eat meat nor drink wine or*
> *do anything by which your brother stumbles or is*
> *offended or is made weak.*
> —Romans 14:21(KJV)

Alcohol intoxication is the result of a high consumption of alcohol, increasing in the bloodstream. The higher the amount of alcohol within the bloodstream, the more impaired you become. According to statistics in 2015, an average of six people die each day due to alcohol poisoning, or drinking so much that the body becomes overwhelmed. The body's resistance to alcohol intoxication poison aligns in the critical or essential areas of the brain that control heart rate and breathing, causing the heart rate and breathing to shut down. This can lead to death.

Frequent intoxication can inhibit one's ability to think, focus, be healthy, work, and communicate. It affects behavior and relationships. Frequent intoxication also influences one to become isolated, trying not to disclose habits by lying about drinking to family, friends, or associates, and even hiding alcohol in some cases, whether it be at home or work. The hazardous harm of alcohol poisoning to the body begins as a craving for alcohol. This chain reaction is similar to the body becoming tired and fatigued. It demands sleep, which you cannot control; you must get sleep or pass out.

The craving or urge to drink may be triggered by internal or external factors. Attention and insight or consciousness to what triggers the urge to drink is an advantage to assist in controlling the alcohol beverage volume (ABV) consumed. As mentioned in the beginning, intoxication poison is not pleasurable, and intoxication is unhealthy, so has this habit of excessive drinking become an uncontrollable addiction? My rap song is "You Are Hooked," and the chorus is:

Un-for-gettable, un-for-gettable, un-for-gettable
You have made me your number-one love
You take me with you like a shadow
You hold me with such a grasping hold of touch
I am yours, and you live just to be with me!

RISK FACTORS OF ALCOHOL

Reality is a hard hitter and a definite strikeout. Consequences and penalties exist!

Many times with a toast, alcohol is the toaster to recognize an individual or group of individuals. Toasts with alcohol can lead the way to consumption of more alcohol. There is a cliché that friends don't let friends drive drunk. Well, when the friend is seeing through eyes of alcohol themselves, who becomes the helper? Drinking and driving is a serious violation of the law. Risk factors are costly, expensive, and devastating. Risk factors include but are not limited to:

- **Driving Under the Influence (DUI):** Driving under the influence of alcohol is prohibited by law and punishable by law. Consequences for illegally operating a vehicle while under the influence of alcohol can result in imprisonment, fines, community service, and limited operating driving privileges. These factors are enforced under misdemeanor offenses based on the merits and history of the first-time offense. If the blood alcohol concentration (BAC) is above .08 percent while driving a vehicle, one can be arrested.

- **Driving While Intoxicated (DWI):** Driving while intoxicated is also prohibited by law and is punishable by law. DUI and DWI are related, and both are violations that have penalties. Multiple DUI or DWI fines can range from $2,000 or more, as can imprisonment, depending on the state in which the violation occurred. The violation is governed under gross misdemeanor or felony. Factors include the subject's past history, accidents, and drug use. Related obligations imposed are rate of operating a vehicle insurance increase, storage and towing fees, attorney fees, DUI classes, restitution, possible criminal and court fees, a scarred background record, possible driver's license suspension, or revocation of the driver's license.

- **Accidents:** According to a National Institution on Drug Abuse report, "Drinking and driving can add up to tragic ending. In the U.S. about 4300 people under the age 21 die each year from injuries caused by underage drinking, more than 35 percent in car crashes."

- **Relationships:** Relationships are valued connections, resources, positive interactions, and communications, and socially are viewed as binding or a bond. When a relationship becomes troubled, an uncomfortable strain affects the stability of comfort and sometimes trust. Drugs, for instance, can cause damage to a good relationship with family, friends, and acquaintances. Relationships should be positive, supportive, and loving.

- **Jail:** A sentence for punishment of an unlawful crime.

- **Divorce:** Divorce can carry the burden of a setback. Change is transition and is sometimes stressful. An individual can feel pressure and seek relief that may eventually lead to depression, anxiety, or harmful opioids without medical advice.

- **License suspension:** A period of time in which a valid driver's license privilege is suspend temporarily.

- **Financial burden:** Fines, fees, loss of driving privileges, and other costly expenses create a financial burden or loss of income that may be saved or distributed differently.

- **Health issues:** The quote "Your health is wealth" has merit and is valuable. Your health matters, and chemical dependency addiction impairs the body system with side effects such as strokes, hypertension, seizers, respiratory problems, and heart failure.

- **Employment:** The Employment Assistance Program (EAP) is an employment assistance agency providing services to assist in personal, financial, and work-related occurrences.

- **Court-ordered rehabilitation:** The risk factors associated with alcohol-related court can be positive. The individual who takes advantage of this opportunity could overcome alcohol addiction and improve his or her behavior to become a more productive citizen. This also helps one to rebuild their lives. Alcohol rehabilitation also allows people to heal from addiction and dependence issues. Most people prefer alcohol rehabilitation programs to avoid criminal sentencing and to get their lives back on track. Risk factors can work out very well for one and help one get his or her positive life back.

- **Child neglect:** Families and especially children struggle and suffer as they learn to live without your guidance. Being absent in your children's lives signals a lack of love and trust for them. They begin to doubt themselves despite your habit of addiction.

- **Grief:** There is regret and self-punishment for the injury, harm, or death inflicted upon another while impaired by the use of alcohol (drinking and driving).

ALCOHOLICS ANONYMOUS TWELVE STEPS TO ALCOHOL RECOVERY

We:

1. Admit we are powerless over alcohol—that our lives had become unmanageable.

2. Came to believe that a power greater than ourselves could restore us to sanity.

3. Made a decision to turn our will and our lives over to care of God as we understood him.

4. Made a searching and fearless moral inventory of ourselves.

5. Admitted to God, ourselves, and to another person/human being the exact nature of our wrongs.

6. Were entirely ready to have God remove all these defects of character.

7. Humbly asked him to remove our shortcomings.

8. Made a list of all persons we had harmed and became willing to make amends to them all.

9. Made direct amends to such people whenever possible, except when to do so would injure them or others.

10. Continued to take personal inventory and when we were wrong, promptly admitted it.

11. Sought through prayer and meditation to improve our conscious contact with God as we understood him, praying only for knowledge of his will for us and the power to carry that out.

12. Having had a spiritual connection as the result of these steps, tried to carry this message to alcoholics, and to practice the principles in our affairs.

The foreword in *Alcoholics Anonymous* first appeared in April 1939. The first one hundred pages of the book are original. The publication of *Alcoholics Anonymous* is believed to help many individuals in their challenge to recover to a healthy, productive, and normal life. During the recovery process and beyond the recovery process, members of Alcoholics Anonymous must admit or confess they are an alcoholic. Each step of the twelve-step program is to be followed in sequence. It is suggested that steps in program are not skipped. Some debates and beliefs are contrary to accuracy of the twelve steps; however, the twelve steps are still known as a supportive process to recovery and rehabilitation.

Alcohol consumption that seems to create addiction is listed here:

- Drinking no matter what
- Alcohol becoming an everyday companion and obsession
- Binge drinking
- Being drunk or frequently intoxicated
- Being a functional alcoholic

Binge drinking can cause vomiting, blackouts, and even death. It is reported that binge drinking often begin between the ages of eighteen and thirty-four. Binge drinking is popular among college students and other students. Binge drinking is considered hazardous. Binge drinking is defined as the consumption of drinking alcohol excessively within a single session.

Functional alcoholics do not seem to engage in abuse of alcohol. Alcoholism does not prevent a functional alcoholic from doing activities or normal tasks; however, it does have an effect on health.

Alcohol Story

Twenty-seven-year-old female
Active alcohol user
Not in counseling
Verbatim confession
Person desires to remain anonymous

> Alcohol was never a drug as much as it was a gateway drug or a crutch. I knew alcohol made me not care, and caring was something I did too much of, which was why I had anxiety. The first time I remember using alcohol as a way to cope with anxiety was in college and I had a

presentation. I drank the bottle of vodka after my presentation because I felt I didn't do a great job. I used alcohol as a secondhand drug. While using drugs, I used alcohol to calm down or taper down the effect of drugs. I haven't really found a nice balance with alcohol, but I think that balance comes from within. I'd say most if not all my friends have had a DUI or know someone who has died from an alcohol-related death. And I know any time I've wanted to die, I usually buy alcohol so if I do try to commit suicide, I don't cherish alcohol nut I like alcohol. Alcohol isn't the best way to self-medicate, but we still use it knowing the side effects.

PART TWO:

Reality's Portrait Is Pictured in a
Glass Frame until the Glass Is Broken
or Shattered

WELCOME: I AM METHAMPHETAMINE

I can put you on a chain leash, and each time you try to pull away, I can yank you back to me. I am your pleasure, and you become my hostage.

Hey, hey! I am methamphetamine. I provide pleasure before pain. I guarantee a fall that will make you lay flat on your back struggling to get up, if you test me.

I am the test that will flunk your life from pleasure to a ball of confusion and corruption. I am made to pass and upgrade you to a high level of pleasure and then reduce you to a bottom level of misery and plague you with torment. My celebrity name is methamphetamine. My street slang names are crystal meth, ice, speed, Tina, uppers, meth, crank, and various other names. My availability on the streets is disturbing, as are the lives I have crippled or taken away for my temporary pleasure. It is believed that I am three times more powerful than cocaine and among the most difficult drugs to quit; however, quitting is possible and requires treatment. Traditionally, my colors are white, yellow, pink, or brown. As a crystal, I am clear or blue and shaped like a crystal.

> *For he who sows to his flesh will of the flesh*
> *reap corruption, but he who sows to the spirit*
> *will of the spirit reap "everlasting Life."*
> —Galatians 6:8(KJV)

My powerful stimulant can be swallowed, snorted, smoked, sniffed, or injected. I am highly addictive. Your brain and nervous system are my striking targets. Severe tooth decay, referred to as meth mouth, will also damage teeth with chipped, broken teeth. Sores in the mouth are also a common side effect. The National Institute on Meth reports:

> Meth reduces the amount of protective saliva around the teeth. People who use Meth also tend to drink a lot of sugary soda, neglect oral care, grind their teeth and clench their jaws—all of which can cause what's known as Meth mouth.

> Meth users sometimes hallucinate that insects are creeping, crawling on top or underneath their skin (called formication). The person will pick or scratch their skin, trying to get rid of the imaginary "crack bugs." Soon their face and arms are covered with open sores that can get affected.

You see, I am not only bad; I am a super bad celebrity—me, meth. And when my cousins join me, we are incredibly bad and unhealthy! My mission is to supply a sensational, pleasurable high that will make you feel as though you are experiencing a boost of energy, confidence, and pleasure that is more satisfying than your normal feelings.

Disturbing is my availability on the streets and the lives I have crippled or taken away for my temporary pleasure.

Warning: Prolonged use can and will impact your health. Prolonged-use health problems include but are not limited to stroke, heart attack, breathing problems, weight loss, and mental health issues. Anxiety, hallucinations, paranoia, fidgeting, and depression will consume and cripple your life. The body becomes weak, and the immune system begins weakening.

Withdrawal is when one tries to rid the body of substance and the body's response to the action. You will suffer intense pain. The hatchet of substance in your body screams in agony. You become like a chilled or frozen Popsicle melting in the sun, being completely diminished unless and while the substance is removed from the body.

Sunshine and darkness are all around the universe at designed times in zones. The sun always carries light and heat. It is unique in the service provided. Darkness and sun both play significant roles in the universe. They never subtract from one another. Methamphetamine subtracts the body's function and behavior to a negative status. There is no one living who escapes from sun or night; we all are living within it. We all are living within an era of escape. Drugs maintain a dependency in need of escape. My rap song is "You Are Hooked," and the chorus is:

Bam, Bam, Bam
Listen, listen to this, listen to this;
The thrill that you feel
The drugs that you get
Trigger you to steal
Put money in dealer's pocket
While you are high and ill
In body and mind
And oh, yes, I am boosting,
Cause I treat you like crap

The best remedy is to avoid use of this highly addictive stimulant.

Female
Verbatim

> I have been on and off different drugs since age fourteen. Meth has been the hardest to stop because it was the one drug I enjoyed most. I enjoyed it because I enjoyed being energized and happy. I also enjoyed losing weight. I've never felt beautiful or good enough, and using drugs made me feel good. I blocked out everything I felt that was negative with a packed pipe of crystal. I've been around good, beautiful people using drugs and been around good, beautiful people that don't use drugs. I don't believe drugs change your character; they change how you are perceived. When you are looked at as less than, that's how you start to act.
>
> I personally stopped using drugs because I wanted to be a responsible adult and

face my problems in life. No matter the addiction, you're always trying to fill an empty void, and when you realize you are hurting yourself, and you don't want to hurt yourself anymore, you will lay that addiction to rest. It's taken me over ten years. Every day I have to want to be soberer than yesterday. Meth keeps you up for hours, and you either stay up focused on things you have to work on or you waste your life. Most meth addicts are some of the smartest people I have ever met and they would rather do the drug than do life. A lot of meth addicts realize life is hard as hell, and why work on life when you can find a way to get high and let life pass you by? Sometimes drugs can be an easy get-out-of-life-free ticket. But I know I was put on this earth to keep moving forward and make something out of my life.

BEWARE:
I AM HEROIN

I can make it difficult even for the strong to survive. I can provide you with a life sentence of destruction in your life. The bomb is alive, ready and available for activation!

Hello, I am heroin, your earthquake. I will make you feel your life has been chopped in bits and you have no place to go. An alley for living comprises your existence with muddy streets, dusty roads, tents if you are lucky, and shame. I, heroin, a mastermind drug, has forced you to live as though you have become astray. Caution: I am highly addictive! You feel that without me, the door is slamming shut. You are shackled to me, and my shackling power is in injecting me, smoking me, sniffing me, or taking me in any form.

Now hope does not disappoint, Because the love of God has been poured out in our hearts by the Holy Spirit who was given to us.
—Romans 5:5 (KJV)

Heroin is my celebrity name; however, I am also known and addressed on the streets as Big H, junk, snow, horse, brown, beast, dirt, mud, dragon, crystal white, smack, and various other slang or street names. I am derived from certain poppy plants and extracted from morphine. Wondering what my symptoms are? Well, you will experience depression, mood swings, anxiety, weight loss, hallucinations, increased sleeping habits, paranoia, bad hygiene and untidy appearance, and a lack of concentration, impacting your health and well-being.

Doom wheels spin to homelessness, jail, prison, health issues, behavior changes, overdoses, mental disorders, and possible death. I am recognized as a mental disorder.

Remembering the lyrics of both Firelight and Snap's confession in the song "I Got the Power," I got the power to be your master, believe me! My rap song is "You Are Hooked," and the chorus is:

Yeah, yeah, yeah
I'll got my hook in you

The things I made you do
Are frightening and scary
Like wolves echoes in the wilderness
Running in packs to conquer you
It's like thunder and lightning
Cracking loud, flashing and frightening

And not only that, but we also glory in
tribulations, knowing that tribulations produces
perseverance and perseverance, character and
character hope.
—Romans 5:3-4 (KJV)

Male
Nineteen Years Old

College and the pressure of endurance
was like a plot in my thoughts. The plot
scene seemed to say, "Where do I go
from here?" I was tired, confused, and
lonely. How do I gain new friends and be
accepted? I miss home and the familiar.
I was experiencing a change that I
was not prepared for. Parties seemed
to be included in student education. A

party was where I was introduced to
heroin, and my life began a struggle.
Rehabilitation and recovery is now
a vital part of my life. I will have a
different attitude when I reenter college.

PARTNER WITH ME:
I AM COCAINE

To made you experience the tears of a clown and to carry the burden of a fool are easy tasks for me to perform. You are my victim, and I am your misery! Do not mess with me! I am very addicted, or I will help you in your fall downward!

Hi, I am cocaine. Your love for me does not die. I am an explosive packed with ammunition that bears arms to attack and destroy. If you think you are hearing voices or seeing things, it's me, cocaine, feeding you hallucinations. Living with me provides an intimate fancy of romance like connection scenes produced in a movie. Intimate fancies of romance supply me with a gigantic audience. My audience yells, shouts, sobs, and chokes, and tears flow for me. I am addicting and, like my cousins, the wonderful, sensational, pleasurable thrill of being in the outer limits is available. I give you the utmost level of pleasure, so outstanding and risky that it is hard to visualize. A vision of trauma and vision of pleasure; trauma has the greater misery impact versus a sensational pleasure thrill. You see, I am a central nervous stimulant that causes sudden increases to your heart rate and blood pressure and slows your breathing.

My celebrity name is cocaine, and I am surely performing to attract your attention and focus. My popular street or slang names are coke, rock, crack, blow, and a host of other names. Once you begin to frequent my services, I get bored and begin to alter your path of an intimate romance to a combustion of torment.

Health issues are threatening with seizures or convulsions, heart attack, stroke, hypertension, mood swings, lung damage, nosebleeds, loss of smell, nausea, and HIV or hepatitis. Statistics report that I, cocaine, kill over two thousand people per year.

Beware: My performance is captivating and has a five-star rating for activating chaos in your life. My rap song is "You Are Hooked," and the chorus is:

Crack, crack, crack
Lift me up and
I will crank you down
And feel like a squeeze

Busting your moods
And make you think you are insane

My Name Is Cocaine
Anonymous Author

My name is Cocaine—call me Coke for short.
I entered this country without a passport.
Ever since then I've made lots of scum rich.
Some have been murdered and found in a ditch.
I'm more valued than diamonds, more treasured than gold.
Use me just once and you too will be sold.
I'll make a schoolboy forget his books.
I'll make a beauty queen forget her looks.
I'll take renowned speaker and make a bore.
I'll take a mother and make her a whore.
I'll make a schoolteacher forget how to teach.
I'll make a preacher not want to preach.
I'll take all your rent money and you'll get evicted.
I'll murder your babies or they'll be born addicted.
I'll make you rob and steal and kill.
When you're under my power you have no will.
Remember my friend my name is "Big C."
If you try me just one time you may never be free.
I've destroyed actors, politicians and many a hero.

I've decreased bank accounts from millions to zero.
I make shooting and stabbing a common affair.
Once I take charge you will need many prayers.
Now that you know me what will you do?
You'll have to decide, It's all up to you.
The day you agree to sit in my saddle.
The decision is one that no one can straddle.
Listen to me, and please listen well.
When you ride with cocaine you are headed for hell!

YOUR FATE IS MINE: I AM AN OPIOID

No guesswork for me. You will become my victim as I turn your world upside down.

Hey there. I am opioid. You will not find me giving up to make you my victim. I will make you feel like you are stepping on broken glass shattered all over your walkway, and you cannot avoid it. You see, I have the largest fan club in the world. My fans are constantly overcrowding my club. Fans, fans, fans everywhere, just like the sky. There is no division in the sky; it's around the world, just like me. Nationally, I strive and do not decimate. I bet you (even those who may not see me in the headlines) my fan clubs are the largest anywhere. There are not any losses of fans for me as one departs in an overdose; volunteer replacements happen. My fans steal, fight, lie, prostitute, go to jail, and risk becoming homeless for me and will do anything bizarre to get me and keep me in their possession. I am an experiment of curiosity-seeking pleasure with the side effects of becoming addicted.

My celebrity name is opioid. My street or slang names are many, to include Big H, speed, cartwheels, and little bombs. I, opioid, block pain and make you feel calm and happy. My effects can cause nausea, vomiting, and constipation. I am addictive, and my addictive habits can cause heart infection, lung infection, muscle pain, a stoppage of breathing, overdose, and death.

I am in a class with many friends and cousins, such as heroin, methamphetamine, alcohol, and even some prescription drugs. I am highly addictive. My target is the brain center that controls pleasure. I quickly emerge to the brain control center for pleasure and multiply an amazing sensational thrill of pleasure and energy. This sensation is so powerful, amazing, and tremendous; it is unforgettable when one experiences it for the first time. A wonderful, sensational thrill may signal that you are experiencing the notion that climbing on air is possible. Automatic without warning, the sensational thrill becomes an uncontrollable desire, and craving becomes an urgency. You will gain a desire to get me, no matter what it takes. The chase is on for me. Although you are feeling and experiencing a wonderful sensation, the aftereffects are crushing, so crushing that you feel like you have been hit by a big Mack truck, and the odds of survival are skeptical and low. You may also have an unconscious state, which also decreases the chance of survival. I am like a massacre that keeps getting away with victims' behavior changes, overdose, death, suicide, and murder.

> *And not only that, but we also glory in*
> *tribulations, Knowing that tribulations produces*
> *perseverance.*
> —Romans 5:3 (KJV)

Bombshell: Using me is "chasing the dragon" and is an extreme sign that you need help and that I have become the conductor of your life and mastermind. Your fate is mine, and I am your pleasure pimp, taking you on a journey of chaos. My rap song is "You Are Hooked," and the chorus is:

> Cling, cling, cling to me
> You are hooked
> and
> I will kick you to the curb
> Stomp you to the ground
> And leave you wobbling in a pit

Male
Twenty-Four Years Old

Running away from myself, I guess.
Sitting in dark closets alone, just to get
high. Darkness felt secret. Darkness
rid me of confrontations and exposure.
I enjoyed the darkness and my secret
thoughts. My thoughts were pleasing
to me, and drugs made me feel good
about my thoughts in the beginning.
Disaster strikes my body, and I become
ill. I need help! I was prey, like a patch
of wild wolves seeking prey. I need help!
Counseling has improved my focus and
awareness. I am out of the closet.

DETOX: GUT INVADER

Scrub cleaner—seems as though everything is in it: diarrhea, vomiting, chronic pain, screams, shivers, trembling, tears, poison, fear, et cetera. Plus, the feeling of being slapped by unlimited tons of bricks.

Greetings, my friend; now it's my turn. I am Mr. Detox. Please, no screaming! You are not my fan!

It is *pit-i-ful* to see you scream in agony with choking sobs and pain, body shaking, sweating like hail falling from sky, and trembling like the scene in a vicious horror movie. Wow, and wow, that is scary, wrestling, tackling, and being bombarded with fear. My job will bring you chronic pain; however, it is essential and necessary that I rid or remove toxic substances from your body's systems. Why all the terror of disgust? It sounds like mumbling tunes echoing from a broken microphone needing repair.

Why are you crying and screaming like a wet baby that wants its bottle?

Withdrawal symptoms are alive, and I become your rescuer; on the road to recovery, the first step is cleansing the body's systems to rid the body of toxins. Detox is like a fitness workout; it's painful, exhausting, and rigid. However, results become visible or noticeable. Additionally, there are no limits to the number of treatments per year to allow detoxification.

Treatment can require medications, inpatient care, or outpatient programs. Programs are structured according to patient history, length of use, and drug used. Treatment processes include evaluation or assessment, stabilization and comfort, and preparation for a treatment program.

The evaluation and assessment purpose is to determine through a blood test the amount of drugs in a patient's system. Other information, such as a patient's psychiatric history, is reviewed to establish a plan best suited for the patient. Stabilization includes psychologic therapy with medical support.

The plan hopefully, when implemented, will provide hope and comfort for the patient. The next step is preparation for a treatment program, whether it is inpatient or outpatient care. Detoxification cleanses the system; however, additional support increases chances of recovery.

Side effects of detox include but are not limited to the following:

- Insomnia
- Anxiety
- Nausea
- Body pain and discomfort
- Difficulty concentrating and focus impairment

Factors related to the length of detox can include but are not limited to the following:

- Drug of abuse and history of use
- Patient goals
- Previous detox attempts

> *Blessed are they that mourn for they shall be comforted.*
> —Matthew 5:4 (KJV)

Active detox will continue as long as the patient continues to have withdrawal symptoms while in the detox facility. How you treat your body matters!

PART THREE:

The Shift—Plan, Prepare, Progress, Profit

DETERMINATION, DISCIPLINE, RESPONSIBILITY, AND SELF-CONTROL

Shift your stick shift gear to forward drive so you do not roll backward.

Join me! I am determination. I can become your magnet. Magnet, grab and stick to the applied surface. You see, I partner with discipline, responsibility, and self-control. Together, we function on the idea of "where there is a will, there is a way." We encounter delays and setbacks confronting us like curves in a bumpy road. Determination prompts, and we move forward with resilience. Do you feel me, determination? I am within you!

*Now faith is the substance of things hope for, the
evidence of things unseen.*
—Hebrews 11:1 (KJV)

Determination is the process of deciding to achieve
something regardless of the complexity one may encounter. For instance, determination has accurate intentions,
where knowledge, intent, and possibilities are reliable
components in achievement. When components are
present, my determination's response is to not give up.
Reminder: You have a dream and a reality of accomplishing your dream. Focus and determination repeat,
"Do not give up." Determination speaks and consists of
positive reinforcement of evaluations instead of wishing
or thinking you are not enough.

Discipline is the source of self-control. Self-control is
action oriented and sacrifice oriented. Discipline standards master the act of consistency even when excuses
exist. Discipline limits thought teasers and cuts off other
options that do pertain to your goals. Discipline orga-
nizes and arranges life according to what is desired to be
in a win-win status.

Responsible: Imagine this—I am dependable and reliable. You can count on me to perform or complete a

task or an obligation. My actions pursue accountability and acknowledge acceptance to bond with my promises and obligations. Time management is also a part of my agenda.

Self-control: I manage to withhold my expressions that can erupt in anger. Self-control is an effort over obstacles and restraint that avoids actions that are not beneficial. Anger management life skills training can assist in promoting self-control. Victory is prevailing through challenge.

DROWNING WAVES ARE BEING SWEPT ASHORE

Stop trying to drown a fish.

Tides are high, and waves, forces of life and pressure, keep pushing you out of control. Family is feeling out of control; however, there is a life jacket. What is a life jacket? In many instances, it is a quality of life. Quality of life is acquired through knowledge, wisdom, and understanding. A side effect of learning is knowledge. A valuable asset of knowledge, wisdom, and understanding is the value it has on your thoughts and the merit it has on your actions. The content of knowledge, wisdom, and understanding maximize your potential and well-being.

Wisdom is the principle thing; Therefore,
get wisdom And in all your getting, get
understanding.
—Proverbs 4:7 (KJV)

Wise people store up knowledge, But the mouth
of the foolish is near Destruction.
—Proverbs 10:14 (KJV)

Denial is a protective avoidance blindfold. Even the ocean is in continuous movement, displaying calm currents, waves, and disaster forces. Lessons from the observation of the ocean are symbolic of change management.

No weapon formed against you shall prosper
and every tongue which rises against you in
judgement you shall condemn.
—Isaiah 54:17 (KJV)

Sobriety is filled with the opportunity to promote personal development and achievement. Chemical dependency is loaded with clashes to demote personal development and opportunity for a quality life. Stop trying to drown a fish. Come ashore and expand your quality of life.

GREAT FALL: LIVING ON THE EDGE OF SURVIVAL

The egg white has escaped the egg yolk, leaving the egg yolk without a foundation.

Hear me! Hear me! Hear me! One of mankind's greatest power is the power of prayer. Prayer and faith are extraordinary. Prayer and faith produce miraculous outcomes. The power of prayer may also be called a life jacket. A life jacket is faith abounding and hope active. One of the greatest falls is on your knees, asking for the desires of your heart to be fulfilled to God in his son's name, Jesus.

As a man think in his heart, so he is.
—Proverbs 23:7 (KJV)

Until now you have asked nothing in My name.
Ask, and you will receive, that your joy may be
fill.
—John 16:24 (KJV)

Change has a way of injecting curiosity into its environment. Change brings positive rewards as well as challenges of sorrow and misery. Escape from the lashes of defeat. Scripture speaks to change as a season: "To everything there is a season, A time for every purpose under heaven" (Eccles. 3:1, KJV).

A chemical dependency battle is like a season and bears the fruit of healing.

GOALS:
A MASTER PLAN

Goals equal a golden opportunity at life success. Your success and fortune are in your will, your persistence, and the knowledge gained to accomplish your goal. Plan and write it down.

Top of the morning to you! I am your goals and offer benefits. The best results are achieved when you write me down. I offer a golden or great opportunity at life success. Goals are my instructions to assist you in accomplishing results.

A code may be referred to as a set of rules, principles, or laws, especially written ones. In this content, a code is interpreted as an alert or an informed message. A code as an informed message context refers to C (consistency); O (open-minded); D (discipline, determinatiom, desire); E (every day). Goals are designed to assist in achieving a positive outcome when written and implemented daily. Affirmation are encouraged to help focus on goals. Distraction and procrastination can interfere; however, with discipline, moving in the direction of accomplishing your goals is possible. Be prepared to work to acquire your value. Iron with steam, determination, and an overriding drive to succeed.

> *Write the vision and make it plain on tablets*
> *that he may run who reads it. For the vision is*
> *yet for an appointed time. But at the end it will*
> *speak, and it will not lie. Though it tarries,*
> *wait for it; Because it will surely come, It will*
> *not tarry.*
> —Habakkuk 2:2–3 (KJV)

Goals are a step-by-step instructional guide to assist in identifying, applying methods, and implementing direction to achieve one's desires. Goals are a golden opportunity at life success.

> *Setting goals is the first step in turning the*
> *invisible into visible.*
> —Tony Robbins

Written goals are most likely to be achieved. The effective content of goals should be smart and do the following:

- Be flexible and reflect change
- Be concrete and measurable
- Be prepared in advance for implementation
- Be written
- Be realistic and attainable

BENEFITS OF WRITTEN GOALS

Goals Ignite Success

Empowerment: Captures the ability to believe and become inspired

- Empowerment improves the ability to complete a function or a task.
- Empowerment is developing skills needed to accomplish ones' desired goals.
- Empowerment is personal development, which includes but is not limited to formal education, self-education, training, and experience.

Action: Continuous movement and advancement to reach a desired destination or outcome

- Action is result and movement oriented.
- Action is designed to progress and advance from one level to another level.
- Action requires movement.

Discovery: Becoming aware of something based on new findings or knowledge

- Discovery provides information that was previously unknown.
- Discovery increases knowledge.
- Discovery motivates new thoughts and ideas.
- Discovery is empowering.

Knowledge: Knowledge is defined as the art to know.

- Knowledge is indisputable and factual, has proven results, and is reassuring.
- Knowledge increases confidence.
- Knowledge provides opportunities, personal growth advancement, and promotion.

A wise man will hear and increase learning.
—Proverbs 1:5 (KJV)

Confidence: Confidence is a motivator of knowledge and action.

- Confidence provides reassurance, whether the visible or invisible or the seen or unseen is apparent.
- Confidence provides determination to act on plans and goals and all matters of desires to achieve.
- Confidence is attitude, believing and stating, "Yes, I can."

Resilience: Ability to bounce back and recover to try again

- Resilience accepts failures and challenges, not defeat.
- Resilience does not give up.
- Resilience confronts failure to discover success.
- Resilience is not fearful or wary of trying again.
- Resilience bounces back to explore what is required for victory.

Goal code: A daily habit

- Consistency
- Open-minded
- Discipline
- Every day

Goals may be short term, intermediate, or long term. Taking care of our teeth is the standard to prevent tooth decay, just as goals are empowerment for success.

Short-term goals: Goals that may be accomplished in a short period of time. Normally these goals are achieved within a period of ninety days or fewer.

Intermediate goals: Goals that are between short term and long term. Intermediate goals require more steps and planning than short-term goals. Normally, intermediate goals' completion dates may range from ninety days to three years.

Long-term goals: Goals that are normally career oriented or are major changes, such as a home purchase or education achievement. These goals normally range from five years or more, with preparation and planning.

I have always been a dreamer, I set goals for myself, I look at things and try to imagine what possible and then hope to surpass these boundaries.
—Michael Jackson

Michael's vision and goals were instrumental for him to become a person whom many valued.

Goals offer a foundation for personal development, empowerment, and unlimited possibilities. *Plan, prepare, profit, and prosper* are positive aspects of goal setting. Goals are happy to state or express; they offer a great or golden opportunity at life success—especially implemented, written goals.

GOALS:
NAVIGATE YOUR WAY
TO THE FUTURE

Goals ignite success

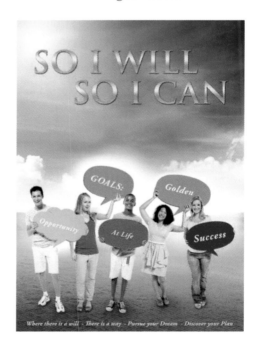

RESTRAINTS, RESILIENCE, RECOVERY

Feeling trapped with no place to go? Escape seems out of reach? However, will keeps pushing to perseverance, resilience, and recovery. Help, help, help! I have a chemical dependency. I also have hope!

The blazing fury of my past fights my present. Moments of being out of control haunt me continually. I am trying, despite hurdles, mistakes, and setbacks experienced. Employment, housing, and community have cast me out as nonexistent to try and live a productive life. I served my time in prison for stealing and now serve time for living. The restraints faced are similar to being buried like a wiggling worm being dug out of dirt and now being used as bait. Yes, I have an addiction and a leash choking me while I am in desperate need of escape. My efforts to escape seem useless, and I become frustrated. I fight to survive; my fight for survival is overwhelming.

It seems as though a lint trap is being plucked from the scars of my wounds; however, it is my will that takes the stand to survive and be productive. Life is like a broken toothpick—a sharp edge without a tip.

Getting off track was harsh, for acceptance proved to be a thorn that needed release. How do I regain sobriety when the craving keeps slapping me hard, pushing and controlling me to do it again? I am your son, daughter, friend, cousin, husband, father, mother, grandparent, co-worker, boss, associate—and I may also be you. The role of the assassin to oneself is not fitting. The highway to hell is quicksand and is a struggle to get out.

REFLECTION PAGE

Implementing and Developing Coping Life Skills

Your experience matters. Write your experience and outcome in a journal. Describe the experience, your thoughts, your behavior, and your feelings. Think about what matters to you and how you can make what matters a priority.

Learning matters. What have you learned to promote change?

Life skills matter. How do you cope with stress?

Develop this page according to your experience and your life changes. Remember, this is your story and life, so it may be written according to what matters to you.

Include your sobriety experience and addiction experience. Review whenever needed.

Goals are useful in accomplishing your desires. Remember the goal code, and make it a habit.

Side effects of reflections are growth promotion and empowerment.

Side effects of reflections are a growth promotion.

A side effect of knowledge is empowerment and a side effect of learning is knowledge.

AN OPEN PATH

The foundation of personal development, knowledge, consequences, instruction, and construction. The path is larger than you imagine. The trail is narrow, and the journey is growth.

THE PATH: GATEWAY TO WHOLENESS AND PREVAILING THROUGH CHALLENGE

Wisdom is the principle thing; therefore, get wisdom and in all your getting, get understanding.
—Proverbs 4:7 (KJV)

Live, Love, Learn

Life's journey—your signature is on it! You possess ownership! The path of life may seem muddy, filled with gravel or stones, green or burned grass. It may be flooded with joy or sorrow. It may lack construction or resources; however, the path is open to develop, follow, lead, cultivate, and fertilize our trail. The path of drug addiction is filled with love for pleasure of choice of drug, trouble, losses, crime, illegal possession, hopelessness, depression, disappointment, dysfunctional behavior, and helplessness. Chemical dependency is a battlefield, impacting the mind, body, and spiritual connection. The battlefield is also equipped with strength. The fight against addiction is powerful unless one continuously works to overcome its chain and lease effect. It is imperative to be open to God's instructions. Residing with love within and reflecting love with a state of consciousness provides comfort. God or a higher power is love, and the spirit of comfort and love is available for you.

Yes-or-no choices we pursue are prevalent and valuable in the foundation of construction along our path in accordance with how we choose to fertilize our trail. Paths always have an entrance and an exit. Small steps have significance and are as valuable as giant steps. The destination is the goal.

You will also declare a thing, And it will be
established for you; So the light will shine on
your ways.
—Job 22:28 (KJV)

The heart has value in supplying the foundation of life. The heart can be consumed with good, evil, or both. While the heart is a vital functioning organ of life, it is also related to the merits of good and evil. You can be having a totally different life based on the choices you made.

A man's heart plans his way, But the Lord
directs his steps.
—Proverbs 16:9 (KJV)

Day and night, known also as light and darkness, are natural resources. The light and darkness are of one accord. Both light and darkness are instrumental in exposure. Conscious of light exposure involves sight, focus, and vision. Darkness exposure reveals awareness, discovery, knowledge, and understanding. When we are aware, we follow the course with knowledge and understanding that darkness hands us, even if we are blindfolded. In the light, we focus and envision an outcome. Sometimes acceptance of pitfalls and stumbles gives us a curve that is difficult to accept or acknowledge. Acknowledge and acceptance pave the way to healing in the path designed to give light and darkness. Exposure is required to reveal awareness and personal development.

> *Day unto day utters speech and night unto night*
> *reveals knowledge.*
> —Psalms 19:2 (KJV)

Personal development serves as an anchor to maintaining sobriety. Patches of disturbance do interfere within the path one travels. The road can also lead to a golden opportunity in combating the crises associated with chemical dependency. Without the light, we will stumble in darkness; however, we shall obtain knowledge.

> *Hear my instruction and be wise, And do not*
> *disdain it.*
> —Proverbs 8:33 (KJV)

The journey and path will have obstacles, and also success; guidance is available to assist

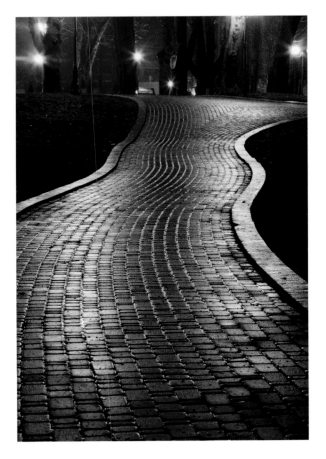

Where there is no vision the people perish,
but he that keep the law, happy is he.
—Proverbs 29:18 (KJV)

TURNING SIGNAL BLINKING: REHABILITATION

Recovery Activation

The start of learning effective life skills is more useful than imagined. Help, hope, love, and pray: the four big four-letter words of receiving.

Preparation is a masterpiece of success. Enough is enough is enough is enough, proclaims the substance abuser. Running, falling, stumbling, lying in the streets, sirens flashing, head spinning while being handcuffed to be taken to the hospital and transferred to a mental health facility, thankful it is not jail. Wow, trips and adventures to inpatient and outpatient mental health facilities are nourishing my dilemma without success. Caught up in a chain, and somehow these thoughts appeared in my mind; I was lingering in agony, reaching out for that sensational pleasure that meth provides. I desired to escape this horrifying pressure that has a hold me. Mental health provides a place to stay, food to eat, a place to sleep, medications, and therapy. However, limited insurance equals limited care and limited referrals, as well as equals a short-term stay, normally a few days if you are lucky. The message ringing in my mind and ears as a suffering and pressured addict having a chemical dependency are:

I wanna make a change
in my life
that keep me from distress
Gotta make the thoughts
in my mind
tell me I can make it happen

A whisper in the ear
A connection to my logic
A desire to embrace
A notion to escape
Deliver me, I want somewhere
to go
I'm starting with the addiction thoughts

In my mind
The blade that stabs my mind
to change my ways and thoughts
and monitor my behavior and actions
by
Taking a look at myself and then make a change

Guidance, goals for deliverance, and escape begin with you.

> *How can a young man cleanse his way? By*
> *taking heed according to your word.*
> —Psalms 119:10 (KJV)

WHAT YOU BELIEVE IT IS WILL SHOW UP

Is Your Connection Believing or Unbelief?

Whatever the mind thinks, the heart will follow. Belief is faith connected to action, perseverance, and outcome.

Focus, vision, and concentration are magnets to attraction and are boosters to the imagination. Imagination continuously seeks expression and is a storage center with unlimited possibilities and wonders. Vision is a perceived image connected to imagination, while focusing is to give attention to. As we improve our vision and focus, we boost the magnet of attraction closer to developing our reality.

Well, yes, many individuals experience the doubt connection. Personalized doubt is a fake illusion.

Doubt is not directional or a positive vision of achievement. Doubt can steer you away from your reality, while focus will bring you closer to achieving your reality. Doubt has the ability to keep you roaming, guessing, and questioning yourself and ability. The logical evaluation of doubt is reasoning, escape, evidence, and outcome.

> *Draw near to God and He will Draw near to you.*
> —James 4:8 (KJV)

Faith connection or bond has the opposite transformation of doubt.

> *Now faith is the substance of things hope for, the evidence of things not seen.*
> —Hebrews 11:1 (KJV)

Wrestling and desperate for a breakthrough, virtue of faith is a loop hold aligned with labor, knowledge, understanding, vision, and work.

> *Where there is no vision, the people perish: But he that keeps the law, happy is he.*
> —Proverbs 29:18 (KJV)

SURRENDER

Acknowledging a need for help. The battle is strong and cannot be conquered alone. A spiritual connection possess miracles.

Being helpless, defeated, fearful, beaten up, and strangled with confronting the string of negative behavior challenges is a sore and wounded experience and crisis, feeling that you are lacking the ability to escape the habit of addiction. Surrender is a strong responsibility, hindering adherence to your will and choices. Will is connected to possession of strength. Surrendering is not thought of as being easy, and sometimes surrendering is not fully understood. Transition to surrendering is an outlet for unmanageable or uncontrollable instructions for a fruitful life. After doing the same thing again and again, with the results having no benefits, and the experience also seems to be chaotic, just maybe surrendering is knocking.

For God has not given us A spirit of fear, But of power and of love and a sound mind.
—2 Timothy 1:7 (KJV)

I can do all thing through Christ who strengthens me.
—Philippians 4:13 (KJV)

Surrendering bear the fruit of commitment, trust, and faith in God (Highest Power). Giving of oneself is the will of God and is not concentrated on things, but adhering to the word of God. Do not block your blessing! Cords of surrender ponder us with free will and diligence. Diligence is attached to our thoughts and actions. Will can thrust us forward or keep us stuck.

Psychological surrender is addressed as being attached to something that is difficult to let go. Focus is concentrated on notion that we can manage the situation. The situation presents itself in an overwhelming crisis, despite our remedies for resolving and finding a solution without help.

CONSCIOUSNESS AWARENESS AGREEMENT

Modified Steps rephrased from
Master Mind Journal, 1998

1. **I surrender.**
    I admit that of myself, I am powerless to solve my problems, powerless to improve my life. I need help.

2. **I believe.**
    I come to believe a power greater than myself is available for providing

assistance and support and providing
what I ask for.

3. I am ready to be changed.

I realize that erroneous, self-defeating
thinking is the cause of my problems,
unhappiness, tears, and consequences.
I am ready to have my beliefs and
attitudes changed so my life can be
transformed.

4. I decided to be changed.

I make a decision to surrender my will
and my life to Higher Power (God). I ask
to be changed in depth.

5. I forgive.

I forgive myself give myself for all my
mistakes and shortcomings. I also forgive
all other persons who may have harmed
me.

6. I ask.

I make known my specific requests,
asking my partners' support in knowing

that the Higher Power (God) is fulfilling my needs.

7. I give thanks.

I give thanks that Higher Power (God) is responding to my needs, and I possess the same feelings I would have if my requests were fulfilled.

8. I dedicated my life.

I now have a covenant in which it is agreed that Higher Power (God) is supplying me with an abundance of all things necessary to live a successful and happy life.

9. I decided to be of service.

I dedicate myself to be of maximum service to Higher Power (God) and those around me, to live in a manner that sets the highest example for others to follow and to remain responsive to Higher Power's (God's) guidance. I go forth with a spirit of enthusiasm, excitement, and expectancy. I have faith, and I am at peace.

10. I believe love is…

I believe love is not blind. Love is an
awakening, and when experienced, it
counterfeits fleshly negative thoughts.
Thoughts of love are divine, while
thoughts of confusion are from the flesh.

*And now abide faith, hope, love these three, but
the greatest of these is love.*
—1 Corinthians 13:13 (KJV)

One of the greatest powers that exists is love. God is
love, and this power of love is extended to us for service,
sharing, and well-being. Love is like a jewelry box. The
value is multiplied by the contents.

AFFIRMATIONS: A PULLING STRING TO SUCCESS

So I Will, So I Can

- Every day in every way, my life is getting better and better.
- I am my own best friend, the person I enjoy being with the most.
- I have the persistence, determination, desire, and will so I can make changes in my life.
- I choose and manage thoughts and words that support and enable me to renew my focus.

- I seek life that removes limits I place on myself and believe the ability to remove these obstacles is available to me.
- My faith lovingly accepts and acknowledges God's will fulfills my life.
- Love is valuable and surrounds me, and I am aware of love's existence and its role of giving and receiving as a part of my life.
- Self-confidence is evident in my walk, my posture, my smile, my voice, and all that I encounter.
- I have a positive attitude recognizing opportunities are available.
- Today is the most magnificent day of my life.
- I give thanks and gratitude daily for life and _____.
- I am connected to God, Higher Power.
- I am connected to having faith.
- I am connected to love.
- I am connected to abundance and prosperity.
- I am connected to being healthy.
- I am connected to giving and receiving.
- I am connected to service.
- I am connected to forgiveness.
- I am connected to righteousness.
- I am connected to being thankful, playful, and grateful.

Love experience: Love will not leave you and will travel with you wherever you may go. Acknowledge love; love has a backbone that is firm and flexible at the same time. I am experiencing the love of God. Wisdom, knowledge, and understanding dwell with the love experience. I am connected to love.

Focus experience: Focus is ability to concentrate or give attention. An advantage of focus is that it improves mental endurance; in order to focus, distraction must be eliminated.

Vision experience: The practice of being able to see. Vision experience may come as a dream or through the imagination, as well as sight. Visions are seen and unseen.

> *Where there is no vision the people perish: but*
> *he that keep the law happy is he.*
> —Proverbs 29:18 (KJV)

Dream experience: Communication and transmission of a message in one's sleep or while daydreaming. Dreams are defined as a series of thoughts during sleep or daydreaming occurring in a person's mind.

Meditation/silent time experience: Art of relaxation. Connection to experience self-awareness. Listening to silence enables self-connection of thoughts of wholeness.

Manifestation experience: The magic of seeing a desired outcome. Preparation and goals are the side effects to assist in manifestation.

Affirmations are the spring board of focus, vision, dreams, meditation, and manifestation. *Speak it, believe it, and achieve it* are the ingredients. Speak, write, and learn; knowledge is a seed of success. Seeds produce what you plant.

STAGGERING TO CROSS THE FINISH LINE

Slapped with setback desire. Do not give up. Relapse is not your ultimate desire. Let drive propel resilience. Defeat me if you will!

Slapped with desire to give in before reaching the finish line, keep on the straightaway of the will that flows with determination, resilience, and persistence to never give up. The greatness of God dwells within your faith/belief.

Secret of Life

Take time to think: it is a source of power

Take time to play: it is the secret of perpetual youth

Take time to be friendly: it is road to happiness

Take time to work: it is price of success

Take time to pray: it is the greatest power on earth

Take time to love and be loved: it is the way of God
—Author Unknown

Endurance is a period of change that is so, so massive to ride. Endurance is defined as a continuous action of persistence to overcome the power of adversity, hardships, difficult situations, and setbacks. The core of endurance is to recover. The stronghold of obstacles is defeated with endurance.

> *For you have need of endurance, So that after*
> *you have done The will of God, you may receive*
> *the promise.*
> —Hebrews 10:36 (KJV)

Endurance can strike out procrastination with implementing this quote:

> *My faith/belief sees and expect*
> *the invisible,*
> *welcomes the possibilities,*
> *and conquers the thoughts*
> *of defeat!*

Endurance and perseverance in their positive states say, "A change is gonna come!" Technology has changed and improved massively; however, principles of life have not changed. Life skills and personal development improve awareness and empowerment based on life principles.

Principles of life include knowledge, wisdom, and understanding.

SHATTERED BUT RISING UP AGAIN

The door to a new life and opportunity is open to me if I choose to enter, remembering I am a person of value, broken, torn, lost, but determined to overcome obstacles through the renewing of the mind. "Yes, I Will; Yes, I Can" is a favorite of my slogans. I believe this message; *will* and *can* are key words. *Can* expresses ability to accomplish, and *will* says out loud with emphasis, "Yeah, I can." Both *can* and *will* are action words to promote empowerment and achievement. Resilience promotes and reminds us to try again and overcome obstacles.

> *And do not be conformed to this world, but be*
> *transformed by the renewing of your mind, that*

*you may prove what is that good and acceptable
and perfect will of God.*
—Romans 12:2 (KJV)

One of the critical elements of life skills is the ability to cope with obstacles that greet us, expected or unexpected. Obstacles seem to shatter life with anxiety and depression, disturbing focus and shifting our emotions off track.

LET'S TALK: OPENING THE COMMUNICATION GAP

Discovery is in discussion, listening, hearing, acknowledging, and understanding. Communication is a big thing!

Gaining knowledge, understanding, and wisdom is not an accident or consequence; it is required. Reach out for knowledge, reach out for understanding, and reach out to receive and ask for wisdom. For instance, the war on drugs is a crisis that appear to lack prevention or control. Why? Because of supply and demand. There is profit in substance abuse market, and the pleasure of the drugs is an unforgettable, awesome, desirable large scoop filled with pleasure, disrupting a productive life with a crutch of helplessness.

*For the weapons of our warfare are not
carnal but mighty in God for pulling down
strong-holds.*
—2 Corinthians 10:4(KJV)

Accomplishing this awesome scoop of pleasure actively involves a secret of shame, denial, and hiding its effects from family and concerned friends. Uncontrollable desire has set a preference in your life, and you have become resistant and rejected admission. A faultless strain to bear consequences of being referred to as an addict is pressing.

Communication becomes a barrier without a perceived outlet. Communication, however, can be verbal, nonverbal, or silent. Verbal communication is spoken; nonverbal communication is body language and silent communication. All display some type of message. Charles Capps's book *The Tongue: A Creative Force* gives a good explanation on the tongue as a creative force of harmony or despair, wounding or encouragement. Observing and listening without interruption are assets to effective communication. Effective communication eliminates blame and pursues information that is supportive to the listener to have more of a responsive impact. Paraphrasing for clarity and understanding shows interest and improves the content of the message from the messenger. Effective communication is a two-way street. Bashing is a critical setback and can cause parties to be angered and be hurt by words.

Skeptical about how to reveal your dilemma and secret? Seek professional help with confidential screening and assistance.

Points to consider for effective communication:

- Show that you are listening.
- Ask for clarification.
- Reflect on what is being said by paraphrasing.
- Wait to speak to allow the speaker time to finish each point before asking questions or responding.
- Provide feedback.
- Watch body language.
- Put away distractions.
- Speak with clarity.
- Know what you are talking about.
- Define acronyms.
- Monitor using slang.
- Encourage the speaker with eye contact.

Speak when you are angry and you'll make the best speech you will ever regret.
—Lawrence Peters

PART FOUR:

A New Beginning Starts with You

RELAPSE

Belief is a six-letter word of manifestation. Do not give up! Sobriety is attainable.

The road to maintain sobriety is difficult, entangled with episodes to activated relapse. Beep, beep, beep! The buzzer is loud, and temptation is high and seems irresistible for pleasurable feelings in chemical dependency drugs. The buzzer alarm sounds in the mind and hungers for a feeding of desirable pleasure once sought. Relapse is a period when sobriety is active, and a craving is triggered for the drug, and the craving wins. The feelings of helplessness reappear, and your behavior becomes out of control again. Relapse is like getting in a swing, swinging back and forth unless you get completely out of the swing and place your feet on solid ground.

Sustaining sobriety is difficult and challenging; however, it is attainable. Depression, irritability, mood changes, and drug cravings are frustrating setbacks while attempting to remain sober.

A relapse is not considered inevitable, meaning that a relapse is not a concrete part of the process. Relapse is experienced by many but not all who suffer from addictions. A highlight of the mind's tolerance for life challenges overrides you, and you seek relief. Your relief highlight is derived from pleasure of the drug, which is only a temporary fix. Sobriety is awareness, maintaining the ability to manage life's setbacks. A trampoline is geared for jumping and bouncing; each time we bounce, we go up and then down until finally we stay with our feet on solid ground. Bounce back to the ground. Bouncing up and down continuously leads to a life of blocking out other valuable events and exposure to life's gifts. Bouncing may begin as fun, but continual bouncing leads to just bouncing and a loss of connections and setbacks. Resilience is calling, "Come to me; I am available."

> *Be sober, be vigilant; because your adversary the*
> *devil walks about like a roaring lion, seeking*
> *whom he may devour.*
> —1 Peter 5:8 (KJV)

Picking up the pieces to remain sober may seem like an impossible venture. Expressing that attainable is a repeated word leading to progress because sobriety is attainable. Visions appear of a puzzle accidently knocked off the surface and shattered all over the floor. Pick up the pieces, and place the pieces back in place. The puzzle becomes whole again like its original state. So is sobriety. Pick up pieces to remain sober, and life's rewards will surface or manifest value of worth again.

> *Until you handle it with grace, it will stay in your face.*
> —Author unknown

Yes, you can! Bust da mood and block the twitch and remain sober!

Relapse Confession: Male

> The thrill is gone for a short time, but
> the desire still lives. The desire is like
> the mouse that's trying to get the cheese
> from the trap but does not want to be
> trapped. Every moment to cope gets
> harder to forget the feeling of pleasure.
> I want the thrill; it helps me cope and
> relieves the stress of life, knowing that

the challenges I face are not relieved with drugs. Becoming trapped is real, and your body begins to speak to you, stating, "I cannot handle this." Again and again you fall short. You think sobriety is good; however, craving is powerful. In maintaining sobriety, sometimes stumbling blocks appear; however, stumbling blocks can be defeated.

GUILT

Acquiring an attachment feeling of violation of one's belief of righteousness; being betrayed or forbidden by oneself

Decisions and choices are some of life's directional guides. Yes or no may introduce uncomfortable feelings that have the burdens of uncertainty, procrastination, and guilt. Guilt may be crippling or may be classified as a healthy emotion. Situational guilt, an emotional feeling, can prompt our behavior into change based on our moral standards and core values.

Crippling guilt belittles our ability to move forward and let go. Situational, crippling guilt takes on thoughts that we have caused harm without intention to someone or even to ourselves—for instance, failure to fulfill a promise to a loved one, and then an unspeakable accident occurs. Your emotions and feeling perceive, "If only I was there, it could have been prevented." If difficulty arises in removing this perceive thought, the thought has a crippling effect. One may experience anxiety and depression as a result of crippling guilt.

Wear shoes that fit
Do not hurt your feet
With sores of regret
Wounds of doubt
And blisters of neglect
—Benzena Brown

Guilt
Female

Feeling responsible or regretful for a perceived offense, real or imaginary. Can be part of the grief reaction.

As someone who has abused drugs alcohol and all the above, my comedown was always guilt, the unforgiving silence when my mom would see me and couldn't bear to look me in my eyes. But the feeling was mutual. I wasn't your typical drug addict. I never stole, sold my body, or panhandled. I always overshared my drugs and alcohol, made sure my friends and I had fluids and food and some sleep. But I wasn't nice to the people that loved me. And I was embarrassed that I was using and I didn't have a pot to piss in. And I'd get mad at my mom because it was easier to deal with anger than my real feelings, which was complete and utter sadness with anxiety. My mom did so much for me that I'd get so mad because I felt I didn't deserve anything. And after I'd throw a tantrum, I sat in my head with the ugly words I threw at my mom. I still feel guilty for how I treated her. When you're abusing drugs and alcohol, you start abusing the people that live and care for you, and it's always with a painful statement or absolute silence. There's not enough drugs and alcohol to make you ever forget how you hurt someone that least deserved it. Addiction is painful for and not just for the addict; it gets you right where it really hurts, and your hands are tied. I feel guilty because my drug abuse didn't just take me down a horrible path; I also had my mom along for the ride with her hands tied.

FAMILY SPILLOVER

Many experience the services of a medical professional for an illness or disease in our lifetime. Some of us are accompanied by family or friends to acquire medical services needed. An illness can make us feel weak and sometimes helpless. We visit a physician on a regular basis, routine basis, or a continuing basis. Medical professionals treat such illnesses as eyes or vision, cancer, kidney disease, flu, hypertension, heart disease, respiratory problems, and numerous other afflictions of the body. We hope and pray for relief and health restoration for our loved one or self. The impact of a loved one's illness impacts family and friends with love and concern. Support is given and offered and implemented through guidance, instructions from a medical professional to family. Learning of an illness for a family member or friend or self-illness is afflicting or harming and is difficult, painful, and sensitive.

Mental health and chemical dependency confront the same battle of affliction, and medical services are needed. The victim has become helpless, and choices made are unreasonable while the victim is in a state of denial or abusing drugs.

Approaching a loved one with a chemical dependency is difficult and sensitive; however, support expressing concern and love is needed. Medical professionals can provide some clarity and guidance on the approach to inform the addicted loved one of the family concerns and actions needed to correct behavior and disease, although the loved one may be resistant to treatment. Family intervention may persuade and influence a loved one with an addiction to get treatment. An intervention of family or a friend's suggestion is to acquire an interventionist professional whose goal is to mediate a nonthreatening awareness to the afflicted family member or friend to offer influence and persuasion to the addicted loved one. Bashing by family and friends has a negative side effect and should be avoided. Bashing is communicating a fault rather than being concerned and caring and resolving an issue.

A plan is structured to meet the needs of the afflicted addict; information is gathered to support the plan. A team of trusted, supportive family or friends is organized (a small group is preferred) to decide on consequences and treatment authorized, and express concerns and benefits treatment offer. The best results for intervention are with sobriety of the afflicted during intervention. Remember, the addict also has a responsibility, and your control is limited to support or a court order if warranted, based on whether the addict is suicidal or may cause harm to others.

Of how much more value then is a man than a sheep? Therefore, it is lawful to do good on the Sabbath.
—Matthew12:12 (KJV)

Grandmother Confession:
(Names are withheld due to sensitive information)

> It is without a doubt that grandchildren have a bond and a special connection with grandparents that are active in their life. I believe that my grandchildren and I share a special bond. Upon learning, although within I knew my grandson's behavior had changed and something in his life was out of order, it was difficult for me to acknowledge. A substance abuse

addiction. How did that happen? We shared a household, and I did not drink or use any other drugs. My grandson referred to me as Miss Goodie Two Shoes, whatever that means. I was not pleased to hear him call me Miss Goodie Two Shoes.

In the beginning, I was overwhelmed with shame. This young man was untidy, rude, and a thief. Tears did not change what he and I were going through. Little to no understanding added to the dilemma of confusion of chemical dependency addiction.

Some describe episodes of grief as brokenhearted. For me it was pressure in the cage of the chest, heart pounding, head aching, and sob choking. I became terrified of my grandson I knew as a child. He did not threaten me verbally; however, his actions made me question his behavior. Hallucinations and shutting himself in a closet and making strange sounds caused discomfort for me. My coping skills can be labeled as impatience. Discovering addiction is a mental health disease, I begin to understand the curse of this disease, and my patience improved.

Trying to offer help when he seemed OK was a plea without acceptance. I was at rock bottom and advised to put him out by a friend. Believing I had no other recourse, when he would leave, I would not voluntarily open the door and let him in when he returned. This action caused another unpleasant episode, where neighbors would hear his commotion. What a shame that was! Learning to say no was as difficult as trying to open a can with your hand instead of a can opener.

Finally, I began to obtain knowledge and understanding of chemical dependency. It still hurts; it hurts because waiting periods for help are outrageous, and insurance is in control, not the need for treatment.

I still love my grandson and will support him to become clean and sober again. Love you, Grandson; that has not changed. Also, I am no longer ashamed.

TREATMENT OPTIONS

Help, hope, and healing is happening and available.

- Inpatient/residential treatment facility: Helps patients to become drug-free and crime-free to gain a productive lifestyle
- Outpatient: Behavior treatment plan designed for groups or individuals
- Medications: Treatment to prevent craving and relapse and restore normal brain function
- Behavior therapy: Assists in managing behaviors and attitudes related to drug abuse
- Detox: Cleansing of intoxicants: FDA approved lofexidine to reduce withdrawal symptoms (May 2018)

Have mercy on me, O Lord, For I am weak,
Heal me for my bones Are troubled.
—Psalms 6:2 (KJV)

NATIONAL DIRECTORY

National Institute on Drugs (NIDA)
www.drugabuse.gov, 301-443-1124

National Clearinghouse for Alcohol and Drug Information (NCADI)
http:ncadi.samhsa.gov 1-800-729-6686

Parents: The Anti-Drug
www.theantidrug.com

National Institute on Alcohol Abuse and Alcoholism
www.niaaa.nih.gov, 301-443-3860

National Institute of Mental Health (NIMH), 301-443-4513

National Treatment Referral Hotline, 1-800-662-HELP

WAR ON DRUGS

Humanitarian alarm. An explosive blast or a sinking ship. Pleading and weeping for life preservers. I say it loud: "I am hooked; please release me!"

Outcry is real and suicide to the community, family, and individuals. The war on drugs has grown to a level we can identify as a national disaster. Original attempts on drug distribution was focused and targeted on the black community; however, the outreach has grown to a diversity effect. The diversity effect means we are all in this together, despite ethic grouping. Corruption of drug distribution has become a crisis that forbids interruption and prevention and is seemingly slowly curable, despite medical treatment. Chemical dependency can be treated and relieved of continuously use; however, it can be triggered and repeated again, again, and again, known as relapse.

God created man in his own image; In the image of God, he created them; Male and female He created them.
—Genesis 1:27 (KJV)

Chemical dependency is a strangler directed at the restraint of the minority male and faced with the emerge of many females and males. Reducing sperm dissemination and imprisonment corruption backfired and lost direction to the source targeted. In the United States, multiplication and access to drugs was made easier than assistance, employment, training, education, and acceptance.

Once the climate of spreading to population of whites and stealing was rampant among all races, methadone clinics began to emerge to provide medication that would prevent stealing and craving associated with drug use. Methadone side effects are anxiety, sleep problems, nervousness, weakness, constipation, and sexual problems. Methadone is another drug and is regulated and controlled; however, the disadvantage is when the drug is not available for the addiction, the craving becomes active again.

In 2018, the FDA approved lofexidine to administer to addicts for the prevention of stealing and craving of drugs.

Principles of Buddhists for chemical dependency state:

- Addiction creates suffering.
- The cause of addiction is repetitive craving.
- Recovery is possible.
- The path to recovery is available.

Buddhist practice meditation is a part of therapy and does not require identifying oneself as an addict or alcoholic. Membership is not required to attend Buddhist practice.

Although Alcoholics Anonymous principles require identifying oneself as an alcoholic, the twelve-step program is noted as effective and is practiced all over the nation.

Many recovery programs are available that offer help, hope, and healing; however, availability is limited without health insurance.

SIDE EFFECTS

Principles and causes that impact life are wisdom, knowledge, and understanding.

Knowledge, wisdom, and understanding are empowerment. A side effect of knowledge, wisdom, and understanding is growth. Life skills are learning platforms for success, providing rewards and consequences. For instance, the side effect of determination leads to being unstoppable in persistence and resilience. Side effects are widely known in medicine; however, they are also present in life skills of success and consequences. Wisdom, knowledge, and understanding can bring good things to life.

> *The heart of him who has understanding seek knowledge.*
> —Proverbs 15:14 (KJV)

Wisdom is better than weapons of war.
—Ecclesiastes 9:18 (KJV)

Wise people store up Knowledge.
—Proverbs 10:14 (KJV)

Recognize that a substance abuse side effect is chemical dependency, which is addiction. Addiction is treated as a mental health disorder because of the impacts chemical dependency substances have on the brain. Vulnerability and acceptance are side effects that cater to resistance. Vulnerability refers to susceptibility or weakness and damage associated with a particular situation transitioning to potential complications. Resistance psychologically is the conscious or unconscious defense against change. Acceptance is being aware of the condition.

Craving the substance becomes a side effect, starting with the first intake of the stimulant substance entering into the brain's pleasure center. Craving for the dosages increases as the craving is intensified to acquire pleasure that was received with the first dosage, and the first dosage is no longer satisfying.

Life skills and medicine have side effects that impact health and well-being. Life skills' side effect is empowerment, while medicine is treatment and prevention that sometimes may have side effects.

LIFE BEFORE AND AFTER CHEMICAL DEPENDENCY: TESTIMONIES

Confessions:
- Transitioning to sobriety is difficult. Emotionally, I compare myself to other females who I feel are more attractive. Exercising and going to the gym help me; however, many females are petite and beautiful, and I feel inferior.
- Coping and trying to be normal is difficult; my weakness is coping.
- Meetings are needed continuously, especially one that I can fit in.

- Support helps me cope.
- Relationships encourage me.
- Developing my life skills encourages me to acquire a degree in counseling to help others.
- Attending meetings continuously and regularly helps keep me focused.

Turning Back to Memories of Cherished Times: Sobriety Wins

Flash Alert
Obituary
Burial Ceremony

Seized, Defeated, Conquered
Chemical Dependency
Invaders and Intruders

Buried in Past
You really had a hold on me.

Reward!
Prowler Escaped
Victory
Future of Joy
In
Sobriety and New Beginning

Yet in all these things we are more than conquerors through him who loved us.
—Romans 8:37 (KJV)

ABOUT THE AUTHOR

Benzena Brown is a loving mother and grandmother. She loves her role providing parental guidance as both mother and grandmother. As a mother of four adults and grandmother of seven, she has experienced joy, sorrow, laughter, tears, smiles, and heartbreak. Heartbreak is having addicted family members and being unaware. Being ignorant about chemical dependency, she researched, visited centers, read, and experienced the tribulations of addictions. Being in an environment where there was limited exposure to drugs during her era, she became aware of a universal outcry when it hit home. Yes, the feeling of hitting rock bottom was experienced, although she was not a user.

Benzena is extremely happy two of her granddaughters are coauthors and have been instrumental in research and feedback for this book on addiction.

Benzena believes in our young generation and has written inspirational and motivational books on goals for youth. Benzena is originally from Hampton, Virginia; however, she now lives in Las Vegas, Nevada.

She served and retired from Department of Defense. Her services included change management and stress management facilitator, mediator for the Superior Court of California, administration. Volunteer services include the suicide hotline for the fire department, rehabilitation services for the Salvation Army, and anger management facilitator. She is also an organ donor and expresses gratitude for restoring her son life to healthy living for a period. Her son now needs another kidney.

Course credits were earned at Miami-Dade South Campus in Miami, Florida; Valley College in San Bernardino, California; and Chapman University in Riverside, California.

BENZENA BROWN   SADEJA GRIFFIN

SIDE EFFECTS THE
MAGICAL STEERING
WHEEL TO SUCCESS

DISCOVER HOW CAUSE AND
EFFECT ALIGN WITH SIDE EFFECTS TO
PEEL OFF LIMITS TO SUCCESS

WORKS CITED

"Alcohol is labeled as the gateway to addiction and may lead to other drugs." *The Lancet*, 2019. https://doi.org/10.1016/S0140-6736(19)30713-5

Alcoholics Anonymous. Twelve Steps to Alcohol Recovery.- 1939- William Wilson

The Tongue A Creative Force- Charles Capps – 1976

Lofexidine- drugs @FDA information.gov